THE THREEFOLD BOND

MYLES & SELORM HAGAN

Lumière Creatif

THE THREEFOLD BOND

© Copyright 2022

Myles & Selorm Hagan

ISBN: 978-9988-9184-8-4

Phone:
233 24 481 9266

Email:
kwshagan@yahoo.com

Print, Cover Design and Layout by:
Lumière Creatif

Phone:
233 59 6325 643
233 20 3433 177

Email:
Lumierecreatif@gmail.com
Info@lumierecreatif.com

Website:
www.lumierecreatif.com

Research & Editorial Assistance:
Role Model Africa

Phone:
233 24 8417 088

Email:
Info@rolemodelafrica.org
Rolemodelafrica@gmail.com

Website:
www.rolemodelafrica.org

Dedication

This book is dedicated to our sisters and their husbands. We know God is raising armies of powerful couples. Upon all of us, may God shower His favour and preserve our marital glories. May He cause us not to miss any days of visitation concerning our marital glory.

Dr. James & Dr. Mrs Janet Neequaye

Mr. Prince & Mrs Semefa Mankata

Mr. Richard & Mrs Sefakor Ahiagble

Mr Benjamin & Mrs Senyo Tetteh

Mr Emmanuel Nana & Mrs Elizabeth Nana Ama Atuahene

Acknowledgement

Our gratitude goes to the Almighty God, the one true God who is the Father, Son and Holy Spirit, for His great and manifold love bestowed on us. We have no words to fully express our appreciation and thanks for the grace and favour on our life and the blessings of our family, friends, colleagues and other loved ones. We thank God for His revelation, impartation and inspiration to write this book.

There are many to whom we would like to express our deep appreciation but only a few can be mentioned to represent all of them.

To our lovely and wonderful gifts from God being our sons Percy Victor Christian Hagan Jnr and Anael Christian Hagan Jnr. We love you and thank God for your lives.

We appreciate our parents, Mr. Percy Victor Christian Hagan, of blessed memory, and Mrs. Dorothy Hagan . Mr. Anael Glymin, also of blessed memory, and Mrs. Judith Glymin. We also celebrate our grandparents. Mr. Myles Christian Hagan of blessed memory and Mrs. Elizabeth Hagan.

We appreciate the support and efforts of the Lumiére Creatif Team and Mr. Enimil Ashong for reviewing the draft and providing vital insights and substance to our Book. We appreciate all our special distinguished personalities for the endorsements and the foreword. We are very grateful.

God bless you all!

Endorsements

The Threefold Bond

If there is one subject that has been explored for generations, and still remains a mystery, it must be that of love and marriage. Through the years, songs, films, proverbs and books have sought to unravel the secrets of love and marital happiness.

The famous Trojan war in Greek mythology, than lasted for ten years and led to the loss of many lives, was occasioned by Prince Paris falling in love with and eloping with Queen Helen. So what is love? Someone defined love as, "the feeling you feel when you feel a feeling you've never felt before." But is love really a feeling?

In their first book, ***The Threefold Bond***, Myles and Selorm Hagan explore some of the most pertinent issues in marriage including the purpose and context of a Christian marriage, what to consider in choosing a partner, roles of the couple and the tricky 'hot' subject of romance, sex and marriage.

As is my custom, I tried to single out my favourite chapter in *The Threefold Bond*, and I will tell you why it wasn't so straightforward. As a lifelong student of purpose, I was tempted to go for Chapter four on 'Why Marry'. The social scientist and interviewer in me leaned towards Chapter 5 on what to consider when choosing a partner. My storytelling side related easily to Adadzewaa, Akosua and Yoofi in Chapters 1 and 3.

I however settled on the final chapter of the **Threefold Bond** that details the little foxes that spoil the vineyard. I think it is by far the most practical and relatable part of the book. Many marriages have fallen due to their inability to navigate 'foxes' like division of labour, finances, communication and personality differences, managing conflict, sex, abuse and unrealistic expectations. Those are priceless gifts.

I have known Myles for years as a friend, brother and a business partner. Comfort and I truly treasure our relationship with him and his lovely wife, Selorm. It is therefore an honor to recommend this book, ***The Threefold Bond***. A solid grasp of the foundational principles shared in this book will strengthen your various relationships and increase your understanding of love and marriage.

I wholly and unreservedly recommend this book, *The Threefold Bond*, by Myles and Selorm Hagan and pray for it to be a phenomenal success.

Rev. Albert Ocran,

Pastor and Executive Coach.

This one is not like most of what you may have read. The style of writing itself tells it all, that for it to succeed, *love and marriage is very serious business and one which calls for absolute commitment on the part of both parties.*

The authors cuts down the chase and place the success or failure of marriage right at the door step of both participants. They teach and remind us, that there are serious rules of engagement beyond mere sentiments and emotions. They emphasize that one should *not be swayed by public opinions neither bow to pressures to hasten into wedlock.*

They boldly let us know that marriage is hard work and will succeed if we give it our best. That we must commit time to communication and establish healthy principles in the courtship period that will strengthen and make marriage *enjoyable*.

Graciously, they share with us some tools for success by placing God's Word and healthy communication as some key steps to a more fulfilled life.

Precise principles and constructive concepts, I fully associate with this work and I absolutely endorse it. God Bless.

Dr. C.J. Buckman
Leadership and Relationships consultant

D r. Myles Christian Hagan and Mrs Selorm Hagan have beautifully etched in this book the essentials and ingredients that make marriage work. It is a needful material to help restore and build long lasting marriages in our days especially when there has been perversion in this subject matter. This book I belive has been authored in such a timely manner in this present age to help marriages in all its entirety. This is material for all in this institution and those yet to join the club to read to beef up their knowledge in marriage. Have a great read and let the information inform and transform you.

Best read!

Mr. Seth A. Baah-Ansah

The Threefold Bond is a life-changing book that simplifies marriage to couples who are married, individuals planning to get married, individuals who want to get married and for people who are not ready to get married any time soon. Threefold Bond targets all and sundry. It is in no way limited to married couples. Every and any one who seeks to have a better understanding of love and marriage as intended by Christ needs to have a read.

Threefold Bond gives an unadulterated, undiluted view on marriage through the word.

The Threefold Bond shows rather than tell why we need to marry and gives a very detailed list of qualities to look out for in a partner. Romance, sex and childbearing which are topics on the hush are echoed loudly in the book.

The book will guide you through a journey of understanding marriage from different angles and perspectives and will also activate thought provoking questions in your mind so you can see Christ-centered results. Whether your marriage is healthy, needing an overhaul, you are preparing to get married, or trying to understand the concept of marriage, this book will help you and give you clarity.

After reading this book your mind will be renewed and you will have a more refreshing and positive outlook to marriage.

Mr. Delasie Dogbey
Published Author
Ghostwriter
Relationship Coach
Trainer
Impact Leader

Foreword

"Selfishly develop yourself to selflessly serve each other"

– Richard Akita

There are so many ways to approach marriage, yet there is the blueprint which sets the parameters which demands a journey of discovery, improvement, and purpose during the season of singleness. This journey is pivotal of both parties who desire to enter the blessed institution of marriage.

Myles and Selorm dont just throw their voice into the myriad of voices when it comes to love and marriage but take you through a sequence of layered, scripturally sound discussion in ***The Threefold Bond***. They delve into the purpose of marriage, roles and functions, selflessness, and service to each other in preparation for welcoming either biological or non-biological children into a fold of security, nurturing and values.

They further differentiate the requirements of a Christian and non-Christian marriage, by exploring what mirroring Christ and His church represents in the context of marriage.

God designed marriage to fulfil six important and vital functions of marriage. To grasp the depth and wealth of knowledge in this, Myles and Selorm have set the expectation and draw the reader who wishes to go into marriage to assess:

1. Their core reasons for marriage

2. Their preparation needed pre and post marriage and

3. How to stoke the fire of continuity

When looking out for oneself seems popular, and commitment to self has increased self-centeredness, humanity needs to take a step away from the drivers that has conditioned a generation to look out for their happiness alone and sadly, dented the backbone of sacrifice. Those who desire marriage crave for a union that brings fulfilment, companionship, protection, support, and growth but these and many more great attributes of marriage is not served on ease but developed through commitment, conversation, and compromise. Marriage is not a solo sport, rather it gives the opportunity to two people with different backgrounds to forge and build a sustainable relationship that imbues respect, creativity, and an atmosphere of belonging that yields and typifies Christ and His church.

None of these can be achieved alone but within the team.

Winning together is the most obvious choice but are you willing to pay the price?

The Threefold Bond sets out and offers the base for anyone desiring to improve their marriage relationship or those about to enter.

This book is a great tool for anyone who desires to know and live out the essentials of God's plan for marriage. It is in this spirit that I commend ***The Threefold Bond*** to you. I pray that as you read you will encounter the truths that will set your marriage as the mirror that embodies as well as reflects Christ and His church.

Mr. Richard Akita

Relationship Coach

Table Of Contents

Introduction

Love is one of the most talked about topics of all time. Books have been written extensively on it. Many great and budding musicians have composed songs about it. Speakers and preachers have tried dissecting it to make it less confusing to our human minds. The core theme of the Bible is love. The *Song of Songs* or *Songs of Solomon* is a whole book dedicated to explain and show the depths and intricacies of the mystery called love.

As humans, we can only try. Unfortunately, the Christian marriage, which is supposed to be the light in this dark world, seems to be failing many. The high rate of divorce, unhappiness and misery in marriage these days, is a huge challenge to the body of Christ. It is time to go back to the fundamentals of marriage. To the garden of Eden where it all began. To God, who saw us and loved us and gave Himself for us. We need to go back to the manual for marriage.

This is what the **Threefold Bond** does. It gives an unadulterated, undiluted view of marriage through the word. The last days are here and the enemy knows; hence, his attack on marriage. The **Threefold Bond** targets all and sundry. It is in no way limited to married couples. Every and anyone who seeks to have a better understanding of love and marriage as intended by Christ needs to have a read.

The first chapter takes the reader through the general overview of marriage and what it means in many geographical contexts. It goes on to explain marriage in the Christian context, thus laying the foundation for the next chapter which delves into what it really means to have a Christian marriage. This is where the conversation gets real with hot truths brought together with the intention to rock some of your previously held notions and sear through all society has made us to believe over the years. Absolutely necessary, previously or often overlooked nuggets are proffered and expounded upon.

Using everyday language and practical stories, the *Threefold Bond* shows, rather than tell, why we need to marry and gives a very detailed list of qualities to look out for in a partner. Romance, sex and childbearing, topics which have been on the hush by society, are echoed loudly in the book. With a whole chapter dedicated to these topics, the beauty of romance, as Christ intended it, is made evident.

The *Threefold Bond* throws light on areas in marriage that are generally ignored, identifies the little foxes that ruin the vineyard and suggests how to catch them. I hope that by the time you turn over the last page, your mind would have been renewed, giving you a more refreshing, positive outlook on marriage. Be blessed as you enjoy the pages.

CHAPTER 1

Marriage: A General Overview

Nana was a dynamic, fun-loving and industrious gentleman with a focus and very determined to succeed. He enjoyed every bit of life and made time to have fun. He believed there was more to life than following a rigorous box of routine activities. In short, life should be fulfilling and exciting. His friends always laughed at him after their usual football match every weekend because he had maintained his bachelor status for a long while. He was gradually approaching fourty.

He could live with his friends jesting, however, the pressure from his family was simply unbearable. He was not perturbed under all the pressure. He strongly believed he will get hitched at the right time. He was in no rush at all. He remained resolute to live his life to the fullest and await God's time to meet his queen. So he teased his friends back when they teased him. Careful not to be distracted, he continued with his CCC life, i.e. Cool, Calm and Collected.

Adadzewaa was a pretty young lady with a promising future. Things were looking great with her job in the advertising firm where she worked. She was a star of sorts in church. Her voice was a classic instrument of praise and she was lauded daily by all and sundry for her dedication to the ministry. You could say she was living the best life; however, for the past three years, she had been on a search, actively looking for a suitable suitor to get married to. All her mates in the choir were getting married; even Jessica, her best friend who had not, in the past, been known or seen actively searching, was now in a serious relationship leading to marriage in a few months. She had prayed, fasted, sowed seeds, volunteered for various outreaches and programs, all in a bid to obtain the marriage mantle. She was tired of being the chief bridesmaid or being part of the bridal train of some colleague, distant cousin or relative of an acquaintance. She had done all of the above, and more, yet there was no man to show for it. Those she came across were not interested in getting hitched. One would ask why marriage was so important for a twenty-nine-year-old whose future, career-wise, looked so promising.

Nana and Adadzewaa are perfect examples of real-life situations. Nana is aware that he will be able to find love soon and definitely at the right time, and like many other gentlemen in our society is willing to wait patiently or inpatiently depending on the situation. Adadzewaa is also one of many young female adults who want nothing less than the marriage of their dreams.

What at all does marriage entail that a lot of people want so badly? Benjamin Frank seems to have the answer. He says, ***"Marriage is the most natural state of man, and the state in which you will find solid happiness."***

The Oxford Languages Dictionary defines marriage as the ***"legally or formally recognized union of two people as partners in a personal relationship (historically and in some jurisdictions specifically a union between a man and a woman)."***

Marriage is as old as time. From the very first union between Adam and Eve, men and women throughout history have married. Across different countries, cultures and people, marriage is pervasive. The rites and processes involved in getting married differ from place to place. In Ghana, the Ewes have their unique way of getting married, distinct from the Akans. Across the globe, the rites for Christian marriage differ from those of Muslims and other religions. Regardless of the differences in the culture and marriage ceremonies, one thing most people agree on is that marriage is a blessing.

We all view marriage differently. Our perception of it is based on our experiences, world views, values and beliefs. The reason Maabena would like to get married is not the same reason Mawuli wants to. To some of us, marriage is a rite of passage: you are born, you go to school, make good grades, find a well-paying job, and then settle down with someone when you are ready. To others, marriage is a reward of sorts for dating a partner for so long, thus they patiently but eagerly wait and endure many years of dating in hope that the question will be popped and a ring will be put on the finger. We also have those that treat marriage as business and nothing else. They marry to keep the family name and business. They marry to get themselves out of poverty. These people see marriage as a poverty alleviation program of sorts. There are also those getting married to placate their parents or friends. This set of people are tired of the constant pressure and have finally caved in. Now we move to the famous group: the love birds. These declare by heaven and earth that they've found love and cannot live without each other. We could go on and on with the reasons why two people want to settle down. The question still remains: what is marriage and why is everyone getting married? (At least, one out of all the people you know displays a "save the date" photograph each week on their WhatsApp status)

We will say marriage is a union of a man and woman who decide to share a lifetime together till God's divine time of dissolution (death).

It is a means to learn about your partner, share ideas and work together to fulfill each other's purpose, help and support each other to fulfill the divine destiny.

Notice that none of the definitions states that staying with a boyfriend or girlfriend is marriage. The proposal is not marriage: his proposal to you in front of your friends and family is not marriage. Knowing your partner's mother or entire family is not marriage. Wearing his engagement ring is not marriage. (Engagement here does not mean customary marriage, as we call it in Ghana). In Ghana, what we term 'knocking' is not marriage. It is the beginning of the marriage process but not the marriage itself. Marriage is a lifelong journey that requires you to give your all. From my definition, you would realize marriage is hard work. How can you still possibly learn about your partner after marriage? To most of us, we assume the dating or courtship period is where all the hard work is. How wrong we are!

We would like us to take note that the laws of Ghana recognize three types of marriage: marriage under the ordinance, Islamic marriage, and customary marriage. With the exception of marriage under the ordinance, all other marriages allow polygamy.

Another thing that is fast gaining traction is the belief that marriage is the wedding. You couldn't be more wrong in that belief. No matter how big, lavish or extravagant a wedding ceremony is, it does not guarantee a beautiful marriage. The ceremony is a beautiful event that symbolizes the beginning of your marriage.

If we all agree that marriage is a blessing, then why does divorce persist? Why are we constantly hearing gory tales of marriages; Christian marriages, for that matter? The Ghana Living Standards Survey Round 6 (GLSS6, p.8) revealed that divorced and separated persons accounted for 5.6% of the population covering the census period 2008-2013. What is happening to our marriages? Marriage is one of the fundamental units of every society. We cannot sit and watch aloof as the building block of society breaks down. To those who argue that we can make children without necessarily getting married, we say, yes, we can, but at what cost? The family makes, nurtures, cares for, and trains up children to make them responsible, well-mannered citizens of the state. Before you think of it, yes, there are single parents who have raised fine children; however, studies show us that it is a Herculean task and that such children may become social deviants. What can be done then? Let's go back to the drawing board. Let us have a look at the blueprint of marriage as the architect designed it.

Marriage in the Christian Context

"And the Lord God said, it is not good that the man should be alone; I will make him a help meet for him."

Genesis 2:18(KJV)

God, in His infinite wisdom, did not want man to be alone. He designed companionship as a need of man. It comes as no wonder, therefore, that man craves companionship. Marriage is the perfect answer to the companionship need which cries out within us. Marriage is an institution designed and ordained by God, as found in the Bible. To enjoy this wonderful gift, we must adhere to the blueprint by the Designer.

A Christian marriage is a life-long covenant, strictly between one man and one woman. **Genesis 2:21-24** says that;

"And the Lord God caused a deep sleep to fall on Adam, and he slept; and He took one of his ribs, and closed up the flesh in its place.

Then the rib which the Lord God had taken from man He made into a woman, and He brought her to the man.

And Adam said: "This is now bone of my bones and flesh of my flesh; she shall be called Woman because she was taken of Man".

God made ONE WOMAN and brought her to ONE MAN. He did not make two women for one man or one woman for two men. He also did not make a man for Adam; neither did He make the woman for another woman.

This marriage models the relationship between Christ and the Church; that is our guide for a successful marriage. If that is our compass to navigate through marriage, then what should a Christian marriage look like?

1 Corinthians 1:18 reads, *"For the preaching of the cross is to them that perish foolishness; but unto us which are saved it is the power of God."*

Christian marriage is not the popular opinion when it comes to marriage. When we say a Christian marriage, we are not referring to the numerous weddings taking place every weekend in our churches. We are referring to a marriage that emulates Christ and the Church. This marriage is not based on what society thinks is right nor our personal beliefs and convictions. It is based on the Word of God and His purpose for marriage. John Stange puts it perfectly: ***"Have a good and godly marriage that shows the world Christ's love through how you sacrificially love and serve one another."***

Now let's look at what makes a Christian marriage.

- Commitment before God

A Christian marriage is one that God bears witness to. Here is how. A couple presents themselves before God and exchanges marital vows in His presence, making God a witness to their marriage. This is a primary reason why many churches encourage couples to have their marriage ceremonies in the church or invite a man of God to bless the union wherever they are having it. In His presence, they exchange vows they are bound to for the rest of their lives.

Malachi 2:14 says that *"…because the Lord was witness between you and the wife of your youth"*. Couples cannot meet each other, exchange some 'sweet words' to each other and say their marriage is a Christian marriage. This brings us to the next point.

- Commitment before other people

Across all cultures, for a marriage to be accepted by society, it must have witnesses. In the Akan culture, there are even witnesses by name whom the newlyweds go to in the event of any trouble. For people to acknowledge your marriage, there must be some witnesses. Even for people who want very private, intimate ceremonies, you cannot do without people. In this way, the couple can also be held accountable for the promises they made to each other before these witnesses. In the story of the woman at the well in Samaria, Jesus said, *"For you have had five husbands, and the one you now have is not your husband"*(**John 4:18**). The woman was living with a man, as married people do, but he was not her husband because there had never been a public commitment, so Jesus saw them as unmarried. By law, even marriage under the ordinance provides space for witnesses to sign on the marriage certificate.

- Sexual intercourse

"Done well, marital sexuality can be a supremely healing experience." – Gary L. Thomas

Marriage is usually consummated by sexual intercourse unless disability or other circumstances prevent the couple from doing so (**Genesis 2:24:** Therefore, a man shall leave his father and mother and be joined to his wife, and they shall become one flesh). **Matthew 19:4, 5** also confirms this.

By the laws of Ghana, a marriage can be annulled on grounds that it hasn't been consummated after an unacceptably long period of time. To the Christian, sexual intercourse is holy and reserved only for the marriage bed.

"Marriage is honourable in all, and the bed undefiled: but whore-mongers and adulterers God will judge."

-Hebrews 13:4

Contrary to the view that the husband or wife can withhold sex from the other partner to serve as punishment or a form of coercion, it is not so biblically. In the context of marriage, neither husband nor wife is supposed to deny each other sex. As the Bible puts it in **1 Corinthians 7:5**, *"Defraud ye not one the other, except it be with consent for a time, that ye may give yourselves to fasting and prayer; and come together again, that Satan tempts you not for your incontinency."*

- No room for selfishness

In a Christian marriage, there is absolutely no room for self.

Your partner always comes before you. Let us not forget the model we are emulating: Christ and the Church.

"Husbands, love your wives, even as Christ also loved the Church, and gave Himself for it."

-Ephesians 5:25

"Wives, submit yourselves unto your own husbands, as unto the Lord."

-Ephesians 5:22

The scriptures above prove that the Christian marriage is based on love, sacrifice, forgiveness. It is in serving your partner and meeting their needs that you will find fulfillment.

CHAPTER THREE

What It Means To Have A Christian Marriage

Akosua has been married to Yoofi for two years. They respect each other deeply and try their possible best to live a peaceful, quiet life. Yoofi is a clerk in the local government office in his community. He leaves home for work at 7 am and gets back around 5 pm. He works hard at the office and makes sure he provides everything at home. As born-again Christians, he expects Akosua to respect him, have dinner ready when he gets home and (in a community where water does not flow through taps or a shower) his water for bathing ready in the bathroom. He makes all the major decisions in the home and believes a man should be in charge all the time. Akosua, on the other hand, was taught a wife is subservient to the man and must not, in any way, disobey him. She sells essential household items to make some money. As the wise woman she is, she always saved her money in the bank through her daily susu by the mobile susu collector.

Communication between them was almost a monologue, with Akosua speaking only when she had to, and this was, either to agree to what her husband said or answer a question he asked.

The picture painted above was the norm some years back, but the story has changed drastically. Now, women have a voice and most people marry based on love, or so we claim. The interesting thing is that our forebears had longer marriages and grew together well into their old age. True, they may have had more than one wife, however, they still had longer marriages than what we have in our days. Also, the empowerment of women has preached the message of women living on their own with or without a man. If our marriages are based on love, that means we should be seeing happier and longer marriages, right? Could it be that we are lacking that essential something needed to make the beautiful marriages we desire?

Take a second and digest this scripture: *"Ye are the salt of the earth: but if the salt has lost his savour, wherewith shall it be salted? It is thenceforth good for nothing, but to be cast out, and to be trodden under foot of men."* -**Matthew 5:13(KJV)**

Are you done? Take that again. Do you see what we are driving at? Let us explain. Believers, Christians, we are supposed to be an example to the world when it comes to marriage.

We should show the world what it means to love and be loved. We cannot be part of the bandwagon bewailing the hardships of troubled marriages. We are to be pacesetters, blazing the trail of happy marriages. But how can we when we cannot aptly describe what it means to have a Christian marriage?

ON CHRIST, THE SOLID ROCK

We have already established that a Christian marriage is not the normal marriage we see and know. First off, are you ready to sacrifice? Are you willing to be intentional in making sure your marriage works? Are you willing to listen to your partner? We are talking both verbal and non-verbal communication. Are you open to recommitting your marriage to the Lord Jesus?

In God's design for marriage, it is only meant for one man and one woman. There is no middle ground or two ways about that: with the legalization of LGQBT being a much-discussed topic in the public sphere in recent times, it is only wise we make this statement. In **Genesis 2:18**, the approved partners for marriage are laid bare.

Therefore, a man shall leave his father and his mother and hold fast to his wife, and they shall become one flesh.

If, in any way, the definition or concept of wife stated above is ambiguous, let's have a look at Apostle Paul's view on this.

"Nevertheless, to avoid fornication, let every man have his own wife, and let every woman have her own husband. "

1 Corinthians 7:2

There we have it. It is not debatable. Christian marriage involves ONE husband and ONE wife.

A Christian marriage built on the solid rock of Christ is not just about the parties involved. As our Master, the Lord seeks to use us as agents of transformation in this world of decadence. He must be our first point of call when we decide to marry. We are royals and our unions and alliances are strategic to advance the kingdom. Our wills are made perfect in His only if we yield to His ways. It is only when we build our marriage on the solid rock of Jesus Christ and His Word that we shall not be shaken. The Bible gives us a short story of two men who built, one on rock and the other on sand.

The rains came and we hope you know whose house got trashed? It is only when we surrender and cry out to God that we can stand; otherwise, no matter how honourable and noble our intentions are, we will fumble and struggle.

• **CONSTANT COMMUNICATION**

"Communication to a relationship is like oxygen to life. Without it...it dies." -Tony Gaskins

Relationships, on any level, require constant nurturing from both parties to blossom. For our Christian marriages to flourish, we need to communicate. When we say communicate, we mean talk about everything: from the bills to how the day went in the office; from our plans for the next two years to that gnawing headache that won't just go away. Your spouse is your friend and just as you can spend time on your phone talking to that friend, you should do the same with your spouse. A communication gap will only lead to assumptions, and assumptions will not do any of you any good. When your partner knows very little about you, his or her only resort is to proceed on assumptions. He assumes the wife is pleased with what he provides to run the home. He assumes she has so much money to spare on clothes so he shouldn't bother. For her part, the wife assumes the man earns much more than she knows and so keeps making demands. She assumes his favourite is still jollof rice when the man has moved on. All these escalate into more serious issues and breed distrust and suspicions. To clear doubts, talk to your partner. Let him or her know everything.

Another matter, most couples, even those that communicate effectively, shy away from is the money talk. They will talk about everything except money. It is an unspoken rule they strictly adhere to. It baffles us how a couple can decide to keep their finances away from each other and expect to succeed? If we have a common goal, are we not supposed to work together? In recent times, we have come across husbands who have properties their wives know nothing about, and vice versa. If a couple cannot discuss money and other related matters, it is a cause for worry.

You came into the marriage with expectations; your partner as well. Have you voiced these expectations to each other? That is another area couples fail. Never assume your husband or wife knows about everything you expect in marriage. He or she can get a few hints but surely not all. Your spouse cannot read your mind just as you cannot read theirs. So why subject ourselves to misery over something that a two-minute talk can solve?

We have a number of couples who have resigned themselves to fate over specific behaviours their partners portray. We ask them a simple question: have you spoken to your partner about it? In the few minutes, we hear a list of everything else they've done except talking. They subject themselves and their partners to misery otherwise known as the silent treatment, drop hints that they assume their partners must be able to decode. Question is, if you found time to use all these non-verbal methods, why not try voicing it out verbally? Effective communication does not mean scolding, shouting or nagging. Talk to them as you talk to a friend. It is a powerful tool in your Christian marriage. We learnt it as a young couple to communicate well and it has really helped us to communicate effectively and share our feelings and thoughts more openly. Always remember , the two shall become one.

• THE LOVE FACTOR

"We're all a little weird. And life is a little weird. And when we find someone whose weirdness is compatible with ours, we join up with them and fall into mutually satisfying weirdness—and call it love–true love."

– Robert Fulghum, *True Love*

How many times have you fallen in love? Once? Twice? How did you feel? We have all felt love one way or the other. The word love has been tossed around very much. In our daily lives, we express love for a movie, that red dress, the talented actress. We even love the works of others. For instance, we know fanatics of some popular people who worship these celebrities. We love our mothers, our fathers, our siblings, that favourite cousin or Uncle. Then we have the "I love you" from man to woman,

woman to man, girl to boy, boy to girl. There are many facets to love. How can one person love his wife, love his mother, love his children, love his friends, love his job? Isn't that one too many loves? As humans, we love like Jesus Christ which is the agape love, brotherly love which is also known as phileo love and eros or romantic love. To many, "I love you" is the firm foundation of a relationship. We have people yearning for their partners to tell them these three magic words. The Bible mentions love 310 times (in the KJV). Our Lord Jesus is the greatest lover who ever lived.

Contrary to what many believe, love, as described by God's Word, is primarily an ACTION (a behaviour based on a personal decision), not a mere feeling or emotion, and certainly NOT a synonym for lust, infatuation, or obsession. Love is constant and does not fluctuate.

It is not a form of reward; you do not give out love to your partner because he or she was good to you. Love is the good that one chooses to do to another, and it ultimately relies on faith and hope in God. True love is humble, righteous, forgiving, patient, generous, kind, and willing to endure personal loss and suffering. Love is the opposite of self-absorption and selfishness, which are chiefly devoted to one's own pleasure, benefits, welfare and profit. Extreme selfishness is one of the traits of Satan, the devil—the enemy of God and mankind. Love is commanded of us by our Creator. Jesus Christ said *"a new commandment I give to you, that you love one another, even as I have loved you, that you also love one another. By this all men will know that you are my disciples if you have love for one another."* —**John 13:34-35 NASB**

"Beloved, if God so loved us, we also ought to love one another". —**1 John 4:11 NASB**

As followers of Christ, we are also to love our neighbours as ourselves (**Luke 10:27; Leviticus 19:18; Matthew 19:19; Matt. 22:39; Mark 12:31; Romans 13:9; Galatians 5:14; James 2:8**).

For the whole Law is fulfilled in one word, Love; in the statement,

"You shall love your neighbour as yourself."— **Galatians 5:14 NASB.**

In **1 Corinthians 13**, the Apostle Paul, inspired by the Holy Spirit, beautifully describes the importance and excellency of true love. *"If I speak with the tongues of men and of angels but do not have love, I have become a noisy gong or a clanging cymbal. If I have the gift of prophecy and know all mysteries and all knowledge; and if I have all faith, so as to remove mountains, but do not have* *love, I am nothing. And if I give all my possessions to feed the poor, and if I surrender my body to be burned, but do not have love, it profits me nothing.*

Love is patient, love is kind and is not jealous;

Love does not brag and is not arrogant, does not act unbecomingly;

It does not seek its own, is not provoked, does not take into account a wrong suffered,

Does not rejoice in unrighteousness, but rejoices with the truth; bears all things,

Believes all things, hopes all things and endures all things.

Love never fails; but if there are gifts of prophecy, they will be done away; if there are tongues, they will cease; if there is knowledge, it will be done away. For we know in part and we prophesy in part; but when the perfect comes, the partial will be done away.

When I was a child, I used to speak like a child, think like a child, reason like a child; when I became a man, I did away with childish things. For now, we see in a mirror dimly, but then face to face; now I know in part, but then I will know fully just as I also have been fully known. But now faith, hope, love, abide these three; but the greatest of these is love".

1 John 3:18 NASB admonishes us with these words: *"Little children, let us not love with word or with tongue, but indeed and truth"*.

There are many more scriptures on love. It is by far easier and only natural to love yourself and put yourself first. It is easy to keep records of the wrongs your partner has done: the world believes you should pay back your partner in their own coin. This is where the Holy Spirit comes in and helps us to love the divine way. He is our guide and teacher. Do you see why we can do nothing without Him?

You may be wondering, what's this tingling feeling I experience when I'm with my partner? Don't the butterflies in my tummy count for love? Well, it's a sure sign of an intense feeling for and attraction to your partner, though it counts for something, that alone, is not enough to sustain your relationship. Studies show that these feelings go away after some time, maximum two to three years (Dr. Fred Nour, neurologist and author of True Love). We must not equate love to physical attraction. Many have trudged along this path and it has led them astray.

CHAPTER 4

Why Marry?

A quote stands out in the movie, 'Shall We Dance', ***"There are a billion people on the planet. What does anyone's life mean? But in a marriage, you are promising to care about everything... The good things, the bad things, the terrible things, the mundane things, all of it. All the time, every day. You're saying, "Your life will not go unnoticed because I will notice it. Your life will not go unwitnessed because I will be your witness."***

-(Shall We Dance, 2004)

Many of us wish to get married and have a beautiful family. As mentioned earlier, we all have our reasons to take those vows. Let's look at a few.

- *To procreate*

Our society, since time, has frowned upon children born out of wedlock. In some communities, such children are not considered when it comes to inheritance. So for some people, when we attain a particular age, we feel it is time to get married and make babies as soon as possible. The pressure is real for most ladies, especially when they are getting closer to the menopausal age. During this time, ladies who have held on to their standards and values do not mind settling for any man who comes their way. The same story goes for men who believe they must get married at a particular age to make children before they retire.

Another group of people who fall into this category are individuals who grew up in homes where they were the only child. These are people who have no biological siblings. They shoulder the responsibility of producing offspring for their entire lineage. They must fulfill the wishes of their parents or face their wrath. Critics of marriage have objected to this reason for marriage. They argue that one does not need marriage to make children. In fact, in recent times, we have seen an increase in the number of single parents, or people consenting to have children outside wedlock. In 2017, the number of children born out of wedlock increased by 40% - from 24 in 1994 (www.childtrends.org).

We would not like to be the bearer of bad news for people who marry just to have children, but please indulge us. What if you are not able to produce children? What happens if you lose your children? Where does that leave your marriage? Many have plied this road to marriage and it did not end well. Why add up to the numbers?

- ***Societal status and dignity***

In our part of the world, marriage is upheld and comes with extreme esteem. Married people are presumed to be more responsible and focused. They are more likely than a bachelor or spinster to be elected into office or appointed for any role. We believe a married man has now joined the table of men. He is applauded as a man because he can take care of his wife and future children. He could have achieved so much in his career, ministry or any other facet of life, yet, without a wife and children, he would not be entirely accepted as a man. There are instances when men who do not seem interested in marriage are labelled as or suspected to be impotent. The ladies, on the other hand, must get married to be counted worthy of respect. A woman may rise to the highest pinnacle in the corporate world, renowned for her ability to close international deals and is the recipient of numerous awards, but at the community level or within the extended family, she is not regarded as a complete woman till she marries. To avoid the disrespect and disdain and even in some cases, missed opportunities, one must marry.

- ***Sexual intercourse***

Kofi has never had sex all his life. In his teen years, he made sure to stay clear of it till marriage. To him, marriage was the only avenue for sex. So he eagerly waited for his wedding which was in two weeks to finally do the do. Many of us do not know why we stay pure or remain celibate. We saw our forebears getting married only for sex, where sex was the ultimate. This has led many to believe that marriage is a panacea to sexual immorality. If that is true, why are some married people engaged in extramarital affairs? We cannot stress enough: sex is wonderful and enjoyable but only within the confines of marriage. If sex is the only reason you are contemplating, clamouring, praying and fasting for marriage, have a rethink. Marriage is not centred on sex.

If sexual satisfaction is your goal, what will happen to the marriage if one partner is no longer physically able to consummate the marriage, perhaps as a result of a debilitating disease or for some other reason? Is that why some older married women hunt for young boys, including houseboys, shoe-shine and car washers even while their husbands, stricken with age, are still around? The reverse can be said of men who are obsessed with sleeping with anything in skirts.

Now let us go to the actual reasons why we should marry? It is divinely destined that man should not be alone and that is why God created a helpmate being a woman. People should marry because they are supposed to help each other fulfil their purpose and accomplish their divine destiny in accordance with God's perfect will.

Genesis 2:18 puts it perfectly, *"Therefore, a man shall leave his father and mother and be joined to his wife, and they shall become one flesh."*

We have always held the opinion that Christians marry to advance the kingdom and do God's will. There is a purpose for our lives on earth for each and every one. For us to make the needed impact in the lives of others, we need to make godly alliances that will help us. This particular move is so important that we need to seek the face of God before choosing a life partner.

In our view, the purpose of marriage is to **lead us towards fulfillment or completeness of life**. When you get married, you step into a significant phase of life that leads you towards a more blissful state of fulfilment. I believe God designed marriage to fulfill six important and vital functions.

1. *The first function is Companionship*

True companionship grows out of oneness of spirit. This occurs in marriage when both the husband and wife can say, "My spouse is my best friend." **Amos 3:3** asks rhetorically, *"Can two walk together, except they agree?"* No couple gets to the state of companionship just by being married. This is an intentional place that requires constant work. We have couples who are anything but friends. Yes, they are husband and wife but they are not friends. Friends take an interest in the life of each other. Be genuinely interested in who your partner is. What are their likes and dislikes?

What are their values? We mostly assume getting married to someone automatically makes us their best friend? This couldn't be any farther from the truth.

Do not live the rest of your life with your partner based on information you were privy to during your courtship days. Constantly call your partner to check up on them, find out what he/she does in the office. Know your spouse's friends. Companionship is an innate need of man and nothing can fill that void. Failure to fill this void through friendship and companionship will mean that someone or something else will consequently be filling this void. Be intentional in ensuring that your partner connects to you on all levels and vice versa.

2. *Marriage is for Enjoyment*

Marriage is supposed to be enjoyed not endured. The Bible says all good and perfect things come from above… thus the inference that marriage, being from God, is good and is for our enjoyment. How wonderful it is to know someone has got your back and will do everything possible to make you happy. Remember the joy that filled your heart when you finally met that someone? Do you recall how giddy you were with excitement? How you could not wait to see them after work!

Proverbs 5:18-19 says,

"Let your fountain be blessed,

And rejoice in the wife of your youth.

Like a loving doe and a graceful mountain goat,

Let her breasts satisfy you at all times;

Be exhilarated always with her love".

(NASB)

3. *Marriage fosters Completeness.*

God designed Eve to complete that which was lacking in Adam's life. *"And Adam said … She shall be called Woman because she was taken out of Man"* (**Genesis 2:23**). Your spouse makes you complete. The differences between you and your spouse are for a reason. She could be the meticulous, calculated type who pays attention to details whiles he is the one who takes all the risks headfirst. Many couples focus on the many differences between them. They magnify these differences and allow a rift between them. If we will stop for a second and ponder, we will realize that our differences complement each other.

Where one is strong, the other is weak. In marriage, we have found the one who completes us and can make us stand out where we would have otherwise faltered.

4. *Through marriage there is the generation of fruitfulness*

God's first command in Scripture is this: *"… Be fruitful [bear fruit], and multiply [increase], and replenish [fill] the earth …"* (**Genesis 1:28**).

The very nature and character of God is to multiply life, whereas the nature and character of Satan is to multiply death. God's plan for man is fruitfulness. We are blessed with children whom we nurture and raise to make an impact in their generation. In marriage, we work as one to develop our visions into realities. Most of us have dreams that need a cheerleader to gently nudge us into greatness. And what better environment to succeed than the loving environment of marriage. Let's take note that fruitfulness is not hinged on childbearing. That is but an aspect of fruitfulness. Fruitfulness means bearing fruit in every facet of your life - bearing fruit as scientists, architects, musicians - filling the earth with our talents and skills. When we narrow fruitfulness to child-bearing, we limit what God expects of us and can use us for.

5. *Marriage helps to enhance protection*

A husband is to protect his wife by laying down his life for her.

"Husbands, love your wives, just as Christ also loved the church and gave Himself up for her." **Ephesians 5:25**

For the Christian husband, marriage means loving your wife so much that you are ready, if need be, to die for her. Christ has paid the ultimate price by dying for our sins. A husband will continually sacrifice for his wife. The husband protects her by praying for her, providing for her, and guiding her at all times. Even during periods that she is not so teachable, you do not give up on her and withdraw your protection from her.

A wife is to protect the interests of her home.

The wife protects her husband and her home by placing them first. They take precedence in her life. She cares for and nurtures them. She supports her husband's dreams and vision. She covers her husband in prayer.

She, in conjunction with her husband, raises godly children. **Titus 2:4-5 (NASB)** puts it perfectly, *"so that they may encourage the young women to love their husbands, to love their children,* to be *sensible, pure, workers at home, kind, being subject to their own husbands, so that the word of God will not be dishonoured."*

A study of 109 juvenile offenders indicated that the family structure significantly predicts delinquency (US Department of Census). Marriage provides an enabling environment for raising children. Parents are to protect their children to raise a godly seed. Marriage is the haven that protects children from the many harsh influences of this world.

6. *Typify Christ and the Church*

Marriage is to be a human object lesson of the divine relationship between Christ and believers. (See **Ephesians 5:31–33**). I cannot overemphasize this. Marriage is a demonstration of the relationship between Christ and us. That is why we have no business running marriage on our own terms. As Christians, we marry to obey the will of the Father as we mirror his relationship with us through our marriages.

With the stubborn determination to do everything our way, our marriages are only headed in one direction: doom. When our foundations are right, however, there is hope that our marriage can blossom. For us to be a testament to others, we must marry for the right reasons.

CHAPTER 5

What To Consider When Choosing A Partner

✓ **Make yourself an acceptable potential spirit-filled partner for someone.**

"A man who has friends must himself be friendly..."

-Proverbs 18:24a (NKJV)

To be successful in your search for a partner, you must first work on yourself. Many people run to the Church to get themselves a spirit-filled, tongue-speaking partner when they do not possess half of the qualities they seek. Marriage is a two-way street. The marriage that works is one in which both partners work on themselves spiritually and in every other aspect of life. Everyone loves a partner who can cover them in prayer and be their partner when they go to battle. It is only when we build our spiritual lives that we can build our marriage right. Develop your prayer life. Deepen your relationship with God.

Sharpen your social skills too. You must strike a balance so you are not so "spiritual" that other people cannot relate with you. Be the gold that someone will be proud of. Do not go with the posture of the perfect man or woman who only has to make a pick or be found.

✓ **Respect**

"Respect is as important as love in a relationship."
-Anonymous

Many teachings and sermons on marriage sprawled on the internet have told us men value respect. A married woman with considerable experience in marriage, once said, everyone needs respect, both male and female. We could not agree more. She hit the nail right on the head. The Merriam-Webster Dictionary defines respect as ***"a feeling or understanding that someone or something is important, serious, etc., and should be treated in an appropriate way."***

In your search for a partner, do not compromise respect. Disrespect in any form should not be tolerated. You are going to spend the rest of your life with this person. How long can you live with a partner who constantly disrespects you? Marriage is a magnifier in many ways.

The vaguely noticeable signs of disrespect you are seeing now but ignoring may get worse. It is only natural that the one you love and intend to spend the rest of your life with be treated with respect.

Respect is a two-way street: two can walk on it. As you give, so must you expect to be given respect. You cannot do things that undermine them in any way. Do not invalidate their emotions, opinions or values just because you do not agree with them. The place of respect in a relationship cannot be toppled by any other.

✓ **Values**

We all have values. Different as our values may be, we are products of our values in one way or the other. With the many definitions of value available, this definition by the Macmillan Dictionary does it for me. It says value is ***"the degree to which someone or something is important or useful".*** Value is an important drive for humans. What we assume as right or wrong is determined by our values. Oko cannot understand why Akweley, his sister, will leave her high-paying job to be a housewife. Akweley insists family is everything to her. To Oko, financial freedom is the ultimate.

The scenario above is but a mild form of how different our values can be. In choosing your partner, it is best you both share similar life values. This way, arguments will be reduced to the barest minimum. Remember, the two of you are not from the same home. Even if you were; like Oko and Akweley, our values can be different. Some couples argue endlessly about very bizarre and funny issues. The root of all the drama is embedded in their values. We are not saying you should have the same values. But it is significant your values are not parallel to each other.

✓ **Invest in the relationship**

Keep this in mind always. Your relationship is like a seed: it needs constant care and nurturing for it to blossom into a mighty tree. Do you want to get married? Super. As you make your choice of a partner, you need someone willing to put in the work with you. You cannot do it alone. Both of you should be intentional about making the relationship work. You will have to forgive often. You will need to make daily sacrifices for your partner. You will need to compromise sometimes. You will need to be deliberate and intentional just as you are with your work. Spend time with your partner. Make each day a new challenge to learn and better your relationship with your partner.

✓ **Honesty**

"Being honest may not get you a lot of friends but it will always get you the right ones." -John Lennon

In choosing a life partner, be honest and pray for an honest life partner to come your way. Honesty is a virtue admired by all and sundry. No one wants to live his life with a dishonest person. Be honest in all your dealings and be open to your partner. Do not alter the truth to save your face. Do not pretend to be what you are not in an attempt to attract your partner. Be true to yourself. Many put up appearances whiles dating in order to get married, only for the truth to come up years later. We can never really know the true intentions of the man or woman we are dating; therefore, we rely on the Holy Spirit to lead us. You need to show forth your good works to the world and being honest is one of your good works. It is rare to find people of integrity nowadays. Dare to be that one person who changes the narrative for yourself, your partner, your unborn children and society at large.

✓ **Keenness on success in life**

Be a partner keen on making your partner's success paramount and in the same way you will find a partner who will also make your success paramount. Be genuinely interested in enhancing the life of your partner.

It is no feat to be in a relationship with someone and you keep growing whiles your partner is stagnant. Know your partner's dreams and ambitions. Ask yourself how you can help them achieve them and set to work. Winning together is better than winning alone. Aim at helping your partner grow. Your partner should be able to cite you in his/her life success story. The success of your partner rubs off on you in many ways. Remember the **Proverbs 31** woman? Her success in life rubbed off on her husband so much that people took notice as he climbed up the social ladder. **Verse 23 of Proverbs 31** says, *"Her husband is known in the gates when he sits among the elders of the land."* *(NASB)*

✓ **Ability to cope with family**

In recent times, the extended family system is gradually fading into insignificance. However, marriage is one institution that cannot do without this family system. From tribe to tribe, marriage rites involve the family at one stage or another. There is a popular saying that one does not only marry the bride or groom; one marries the entire family. This is the reality on the ground. In

Africa, getting married to your partner means making room for their extended family. Marriage is a union of families and being able to cope with each other's family is a strong trait that enables a couple succeed in their marriage. Most often, we do not pay much attention to the family of our partners. If we only know the hassle some couples go through accommodating the whims and nosing in of in-laws! Some couples have had to endure some very toxic relationships with their in-laws all their life. Be that as it may, you will need them as you embark on your marital journey. Do not neglect them. Initiate a relationship with them devoid of your partner's presence. Accept them and get them to accept you too. Remember, you might not win all of them over but it is necessary to have a civil relationship with them. Your partner must work at having a relationship with your family too. This will save you both a lot of stress.

✓ **Intellectual capacity**

It is important to assess the intellectual level of your partner and work at being at the same intellectual level. This is known as intellectual compatibility. Jenna Ponaman, a relationship coach and expert, explains it as "when people are mentally stimulated by the same conversations." She goes on to explain that this doesn't essentially mean both partners should be on the same IQ level. It basically means a couple can engage in deep conversations that are mutually interesting.

This is nothing too technical. Breaking it down, it is what we mostly throw around as "feeling the vibe". Got it now? To most of us, it's not so important, but the reality is that we are more attracted to people we vibe with. When you are on the same intellectual wavelength with your partner, it enables you to connect more deeply. You can open up more and share your ideas with someone who understands your passions and interests. You feel more like a team because you have something to contribute to your partner's dreams and ambitions.

When couples are on the same intellectual level, they tend to share the same interests. Even if one is not as enthused as the other, there is the understanding that "I get why you love this". Remember, this is teamwork and intellectual compatibility will help solidify this. You do not put up the little competition among yourselves and expect to work as one.

✓ **Nurture good friendships first**

"It is best to have a relationship in which both of you can express your feelings easily and that's only possible when your partner is your best friend." -Anonymous

Before a marriage can blossom into a formidable union, both partners need to be great friends. As friends, you know how to manage some sensitive issues and not get to a level beyond redemption or restitution. It is best to start always with friendship. In friendships, we are more likely to know the person for who and what they are. Their hobbies, interests, dreams, fears, insecurities, so on and so forth. We see them in their highs and lows. They also get to know us. The real us. So it becomes easier to transition into marriage; at least, you have an idea of what to expect and how to adjust to living with them.

You know where and how to complement each other. As friends, it is also easier to find a common ground when resolving your differences.

✓ **Anger management**

"A hot-tempered person stirs up strife, but the slow to anger calms a dispute." – **Proverbs 15:18 (NASB)**

There is a popular Akan adage that says "you only get hurt by your loved ones." Recall the last time you were disappointed by that loved one? How did you feel? Compare that to the feeling you got when any other person disappointed you. It is true that when we are wronged by our loved ones, it hits different. Before we realize it, we end up reacting in ways strange even to ourselves. No wonder, news of lovers who have done insane, unfathomable things are rife every now and again. Observe how your partner manages his/her anger. Anger is inevitable in marriage but being able to manage anger effectively will make a significant impact on the marital union.

Managing anger will make it possible for the couple to know and manage any subsequent issues. Such actions make the marital union more exciting and strong.

✓ **Ability to forgive and forget**

We cannot talk about marriage and leave out forgiveness. In this case, we are talking about forgiving and forgetting the past deeds. "I can forgive but I can never forget" is no godly saying. Yes, you can actively work at forgetting. Do not hold your partner to ransom forever by reminding them of all the atrocities they have done towards you whenever there is a new problem. It is not easy to forgive and forget but it is important to have a way of managing forgiveness. Forgiving and forgetting are necessary; therefore a couple needs to constantly explore how to forgive and forget and make it applicable in their marriage relationship.

✓ **Establish trust early**

Trust in every relationship is very critical. It is important to build trust from inception and, with that solid foundation, grow the trust second by second, minute by minute, hour by hour, day by day, and on and on. When trust is broken in a relationship, little or nothing can be done to salvage the situation. Do not constantly do things that breach the trust of your partner. Address any questions or explanations your partner may need to put their minds at rest on any issue. Do not leave things unsaid; some topics are best spoken about immediately. Do not give room for doubts of any kind.

The list is not exhaustive as there are many more to look out for when choosing a partner. In all of these, as

Christians, we can rest in the Lord's plan for our lives. Thus, we should use the example in **Genesis 24:12-14**.

"And he said, "LORD, GOD OF MY MASTER ABRAHAM, PLEASE [d]grant me success today, and show kindness to my master Abraham. 13 Behold, I am standing by the [e]spring, and the daughters of the men of the city are coming out to draw water; 14 now may it be that the young woman to whom I say, 'Please let down your jar so that I may drink,' and [f]who answers, 'Drink, and I will water your camels also'—may she be the one whom You have appointed for Your servant Isaac; and by this I will know that You have shown kindness to my master." (NASB)

We all know how that story panned out. As you prepare yourself and look for a suitable partner, do not forget to commit your ways to the Lord.

CHAPTER 6

Roles Of Couple In Marriage

We are different but equal partners in marriage. We should understand that we are a team. As a team, our differences and similarities together help us win daily. Instead of squabbling over superiority and personal worth and inputs, we are expected to put them to good use. From our physique to our biological makeup, we are different; however, it is interesting to note that we complement each other.

Where the man is rough, the woman comes in with her gentle touch. In events where we need more logical and resolute decisions devoid of emotions, the man steps in. With any relationship, there are roles that partners play to make it work. These roles, when taken seriously by each partner, make the marriage a formidable, enjoyable union. We will be looking at the roles husbands and wives are expected to play in this relationship. Let's have a look at the roles of the husband first, shall we?

THE HUSBAND

"Husbands, love your wives, just as Christ loved the church and gave himself up for her to make her holy, cleansing her by the washing with water through the word, and to present her to himself as a radiant church, without stain or wrinkle or any other blemish, but holy and blameless. In this same way, husbands ought to love their wives as their own bodies. He who loves his wife loves himself."- **Ephesians 5:25-28**

The Husband Is To Love His Wife.

Easy, you might have thought. Permit us to shock you. The instruction is to love your wife as Christ loved the Church, not to love your wife as you want. The standard is His, not yours. Do you still think it is easy? The husband's love must mirror Christ's love for the church. You are to constantly put her first. Sacrifice for her every day. Put her needs before yours. Let us look at the end of the rope, this means that you should be willing to lay down your life for her whenever the need arises. To most men, the assumption is that love is no big deal. Yes, we know you married her because you loved her.

We think this way because we use the world's metric of love, where love is more of a reward and conditional. Where we quickly move on to the next thing that tickles us or captures our fantasy. If we love as Christ loved the Church, we realize our love is a foundation on which our marriages are built. When we stop loving because our partners are not living up to our expectations, our love is not mirroring that of Christ. When we stand aloof and raise our arms in despair because our wives are not obedient to us, then we are loving them wrongly. Are you getting the picture now? This is what it means for the husband to love his wife as Christ loved the church:

❖ **The husband's love must be realistic.**

The husband should have no fantasies about the woman he is marrying. **Ephesians 5:25** lays down the condition: love as Christ did. Christ loved the church, but he knew she was sinful and disobedient. Christ gave his life for the church though he knew her faults. His love was realistic. In marriage, both mates must grasp this reality; in fact, much of pre-marital counselling is designed to destroy the false expectations set up through romantic comedies and Hollywood. The husband must love realistically. This woman does not walk on water;

she has been infected by sin just as he has. She must be reformed daily by God's grace, and she must be loved despite her faults. Scripture says, *"Love covers a multitude of sins"* (**1 Peter 4:8**). Having realistic love is important for both mates because if they don't have it, they will become disillusioned. No doubt, one of the reasons for such a high number of divorces in the first year of marriage is that most love is not realistic.

❖ **The husband's love must be sacrificial.**

He is to love her as Christ loved the church and be willing to die for her (**Ephesians 5:25**). If anybody feels the wife's role is unfair, they should give more thought to the man's. It is much easier to submit to someone than to give one's life for that person. We submit to people in authority though we may not like them. This love that the husband is supposed to embody is impossible apart from the grace of God. To love sacrificially means the husband must often give up other things to serve and please his wife. He must sacrifice for her. He must sacrifice time, friendships, career, entertainment, hobbies, etc., in order to love his wife like Christ.

❖ **The husband's love must be purposeful.**

The purpose of Christ's love is to make the church holy, cleansing her by washing with the Word (**Ephesians 5:26-27**). Christ's purpose is to make the church a perfect bride. Similarly, the husband must love his wife through teaching her Scripture, getting her involved in a Bible-preaching church, and encouraging her to get involved with the ministries of the church. He must seek to cultivate not only her character but also her calling, so she can fulfill God's plans for her life.

He must help her discern her gifts and talents and encourage her to use them to the glory of God. This purposeful love also means at times admonishing her to help her know Christ more. Every man should consider if he is ready and willing to love a woman in this way before getting married. Is he ready to be a spiritual leader? Is he ready to be devoted to the spiritual development of his wife?

❖ **The husband's love must be personal.**

He must love her as his own body (**Ephesians 5:28**).

Every day the husband brushes his teeth, combs his hair, and clothes himself. Every day he maintains his body. Sadly, husbands often go weeks without ministering to their wives. It is not unusual to get so busy with life, work and ministry that some men inadvertently allow weeds to grow in the marriage. Love must be personal. He must love her like his own body. He must take time daily to cultivate a happy home.

The Husband Leads in the Home

When the world hears the phrase, "male leadership," it often conjures up negative connotations, but it should not if properly understood. Consider what Christ taught his disciples about leadership in **Luke 22:25-27**. Jesus said to them, *'The kings of the Gentiles lord it over them; and those who exercise authority over them call themselves Benefactors.*

But you are not to be like that. Instead, the greatest among you should be like the youngest, and the one who rules like the one who serves. For who is greater, the one who is at the table or the one who serves? Is it not the one who is at the table? But I am among you as one who serves.'

As described in **Luke 22,** male leadership primarily means greater service. Christ told his disciples that whoever wanted to be the greatest must be like "the youngest." The Jewish culture was very hierarchical, meaning that the youngest would always serve the oldest. Jesus, however, spoke to this hierarchical culture, redefining true leadership as servant leadership. To lead means to be like the youngest—the servant of all. True leaders will forego their right of being served to serve others. That's how husbands should be in marriage. They should constantly humble themselves to serve their wives.

Christ demonstrated this leadership in **John 13** when he did the work of a servant by washing his disciples' feet. There is nothing negative about this type of leadership. God always intended this type of loving leadership for the marriage relationship, and the husband must daily seek to cultivate it.

Instead of seeing his leadership as being the first to be created and using it to control or dominate his wife, the husband is called to use his leadership to love his wife. God planned this from the beginning. The husband would lead by loving his wife. What should this love look like? Paul teaches that the husband's love should mirror Christ's love for the church.

What can we learn about a husband's love from Christ's example?

The Husband Protects

The husband protects his wife and home physically and spiritually. A meta-analysis of 47 separate studies showed that men have higher speed and physical strength than women. This is but one of many such meta-analyses which prove that men have much more brute strength as compared to women. The husband should use this unique quality to protect his wife from:

❖ Overworking herself

Most men believe they are only to provide for the home. So, the home is a place to put their legs up, relax and unwind while the wife does all the chores. This is an error and should not be encouraged. In this modern era, where your wife is also a breadwinner working in an office as hard as the man or even harder, perhaps even better paid than the man in her place of work, it is only proper that the man helps her in the daily chores.

An overworked wife may get irritable without intending to, leading to arguments, raised voices etc. A refreshed wife is a happy wife and a happy wife makes a happy home.

❖ Verbal attacks

Your wife is an extension of you. Any abuse on her personality, character or any other is abuse on you too. It is not surprising that husbands challenged abusers of their wives to a duel in the past. It is, therefore, paramount that the husband shields his wife from any form of verbal abuse from himself or any other person. Many wives have complained bitterly of bearing the brunt of their in-laws while their husbands looked on.

❖ Spiritual attacks

Who is more qualified to lead a wife into battle than her husband? As the spiritual head of the home; the husband, like a war general, is to protect the soldier (the wife) on the battleground. Cover her in prayer and the Word. Arm yourself on all sides with every arsenal for victory.

Let us now cross the carpet to the other partner in the marriage relationship: the wife.

The Wife Must Submit to Her Husband's Leadership

As mentioned previously, in submission to Christ, the wife must submit to her husband. **Ephesians 5:22** says, *"Wives, submit to your husbands as to the Lord."*

Scripture commands the wife to submit to her husband as though she were following Christ. The word "submit" is a military word that means to "come up under." Like a sergeant submitting to a colonel, the wife must submit to her husband in every area, unless it would cause her to disobey her Commander-in-Chief, Christ. In every decision, the woman must obey her husband, unless his leadership is leading her to sin. In military terminology, this would be called an "unlawful order." Even in such circumstances, the Scripture instructs us on what to do. The wife must be wisely discerning.

That said, submission does not take away the wife's ability to make decisions on her own. Christ, in leading us, gives us many responsibilities and a form of autonomy under his authority. In following Christ, he often does not tell us to go to the left or to the right or when to rest.

Scripture calls for us to be wise people and use the principles given in Scripture. Similarly, the wife may have many areas of leadership under her husband's authority. For some, the wife would be autonomous in the area of caring for the home, even though she is still under her husband's leadership. For others, the wife would oversee finances. Good leaders recognize others' strengths and lean on them in those areas. This is true in every marriage, and may look a little different in every marriage.

This may be a revolutionary concept that a newly married woman must come to grips with. No longer is it simply, "Am I honouring the Lord in my actions and endeavours?", but also "Am I honouring my husband, whom the Lord has called me to follow?" Consider the honour given to Sarah because of the way she submitted to her husband, Abraham. **1 Peter 3:5-6** says this: *"For this is the way the holy women of the past who put their hope in God used to make themselves beautiful. They were submissive to their own husbands, like Sarah, who obeyed Abraham and called him her master. You are her daughters if you do what is right and do not give way to fear".*

Sarah called her husband master, and Scripture says this is one of the characteristics that make a woman beautiful to the Lord. A female considering marriage must ask herself, "Am I ready to honour and submit to my husband as unto the Lord? Am I willing to submit to his plans as he hears from God?" The one who is not willing to submit should consider if she is really ready to be married.

The Wife Must Submit to Christ's Leadership

Again, **Ephesians 5:22** says, *"Wives, submit to your husbands as to the Lord."* Not only does this teach that wives must submit to their husbands, but the implication is that they must first submit to the Lord. The husband is only a representation of Christ's leadership, no matter how delicate that representation may be. It is in submitting to Christ, abiding in his Word, and loving him that the wife will find the ability to submit to her husband. This will be especially true in dealing with a husband who doesn't know the Lord or who is far from Him. **1 Peter 3:1-2** says this: *"Wives, in the same way, be submissive to your husbands so that, if any of them do not believe the word, they may be won over without words by the behaviour of their wives, when* *they see the purity and reverence of your lives".*

The husband's leadership applies even when he isn't following God. There have been instances where women acting in various capacities in church feel they cannot submit to their husbands because they are not believers.

With such cases, the wife's submission to Christ is even more important. By submitting to Christ, she finds it easier to love and submit to a difficult husband and this submission may bring transformation and even salvation to his life. This, however, is only possible when the wife is submissive to the Lord. Jesus said in **John 15:5**, *"Abide in me and you will produce much fruit"* (paraphrased). The ability to love, to have peace, to have patience, to forgive, etc., all comes from God.

The single woman considering marriage must ask herself, "Am I daily submitting to the Lord's leadership so I can faithfully submit to my husband's leadership?" This daily submission to the Lord prepares a woman for marriage.

Also, the single man considering marrying a female must ask, "How is my submission? Does she faithfully submit to the Lord? Is she faithful in church attendance, daily devotion, and service to God?" If she does not submit to the greater, the Lord, then she will not submit to the lesser, her husband. A wise man will consider a woman's obedience to God when seeking a wife. God has called for the wife to first submit to Christ so she can faithfully respect and submit to her husband.

The Wife Supports the Husband

Then the LORD God said, *"It is not good for the man to be alone; I will make him a helper suitable for him."* -**Genesis 2:18 (NASB)**

The wife is a helper to the husband. She supports his dreams, vision and purpose in life. In fact, the scripture says "a helper suitable for him", which implies that the wife's dreams, ambitions, vision and purpose are in alignment with her husband's. Thus, helping your husband pursue his God-given purpose is in essence pursuing your own purpose. If God ordained that marriage, you should not be fighting for room to individually pursue your purpose because your purposes align perfectly.

The wife supports her husband in other ways too. She goes out of her way to attend to her husband. She tends to him and cares for him. She makes the home a haven that the husband is excited to return to each day. Whenever possible, the wife supports her husband financially.

Some wives withhold their monies from their husbands and refuse to support the home financially in any way. They are of the firm belief that a wife's money cannot or does not take care of the home. We don't believe in that philosophy

The Husband and Wife Must Train Their Children Together

Ephesians 6:4 says, *"Fathers, do not exasperate your children; instead, bring them up in the training and instruction of the Lord."* "Fathers" can also be translated "parents" (cf. Aramaic Bible in Plain English). This means that both parents must work together to train the child and not exasperate them, leading to rebellion against dominant, loose, or unfair leadership. Parents must demonstrate godly leadership that models Christ, teaches the children God's Word, and draws them to a closer relationship with the Lord.

> This is a very challenging task for one parent alone and that is why God has given spiritual responsibility to both. Still the husband should ultimately oversee this training, but the responsibility is shared. For that reason, parents

must agree on how to train the child. If there is no unity in the training, it will have hazardous effects on the child. Always portray a united front to the child.

Godly couples must sit down and discuss how this will be done. It will include discipline, spiritual training, academic training, athletics training, and areas of service, among other things. For spiritual training, many parents have given themselves wholly to child catechisms, Bible memorization, daily family devotions, as well as involvement in a Bible-preaching church.

Sadly, what has happened in many Christian homes is that this call for the parents to train their children has been left to the church, the school, the grandparents, the babysitter, the athletics coach, etc. God never intended for these other parent-figures to raise the children exclusively; theirs should be supplementary at best.

Consequently, about 75% of Christian youth fall away from God when they get to college because many parents have neglected their responsibility (Pew Research Centre and USA Today).

Engaged couples should consider their future children's training before they are married, since raising godly seed is one of God's primary desires for the marriage union. Have you considered how you will train your children?

The fall corrupted God's original design for the husband and the wife. Because of sin, the husband has a natural tendency to try to dominate his wife, treating her like a doormat. The tendency for the wife is the same. God's plan, however, is for the husband to love and serve his wife and for the wife to submit to him. They both have a responsibility to raise the children in the admonition of the Lord, but, ultimately, the husband will be held accountable to God for his leadership or lack of it over his family.

CHAPTER 7

Romance, Sex And Child Bearing

For a long time, many of us were taught that Christians must only be spiritual, speaking in tongues and in no way interested in the affairs of men. The "affairs of men" here meant 'catching feelings' or being romantic. This was constantly portrayed and drummed into our ears so much that we found it awkward, even sinful, to see a 'holy' brother or sister being romantic. Not even to their own spouses! How wrong we were and, for some of us, who still are.

Our God is romantic, extremely romantic even. Let me prove it to you. Let us open our Bibles to **Song of Songs** or **Songs of Solomon**, depending on your version of the Bible. Take a minute or two to glance through. Ladies, do you recognize those romantic expressions of love? Surprised? Intrigued? That whole book is a beautiful love story between God and us. So romantic, right?

The word romance as is used today equates it to feelings based on emotional excitement or attraction. This kind of romance is what has been emphasized in popular culture. Music, movies, plays, and books capitalize on our human fascination with romantic love and its seemingly endless expressions.

The Bible has been called God's love letter to humanity. Although it contains harsh imagery and warnings about God's judgment, the Bible is also filled with creative expressions of love between human beings and God (**Psalm 42:1–2; Jeremiah 31:3**).

Love and romance, though intertwined, are not identical. We can have romance without real love, and we can love without feeling romantic.

While passages such as **Zephaniah 3:17** describe God's emotional love for His own, other passages such as **1 Corinthians 13:4–8** detail qualities of love that have nothing to do with the emotions of romance. Jesus said, *"Greater love has no man than this, that he lay down his life for his friends"* (**John 15:13**).

Dying an agonizing death on a cross for ungrateful sinners was in no way romantic, but it was the ultimate expression of love (**1 John 4:9–10**).

The *Songs of Solomon* is a book filled with romantic demonstrations of love between a bride and groom. Because God included this book in the canon of His inspired Word, we can safely say that romance is acceptable and even applauded by our Creator. Romance, in the context of a pure and committed relationship, can enhance that relationship and increase the enjoyment of love in marriage, as God intended.

Romance for the sake of romance, however, can be destructive. Most romances begin with the delightful sense of "falling in love," which can be intoxicating. The act of "falling in love" produces a chemical deluge in the brain similar to that experienced with drug use. The brain is awash in adrenaline, dopamine, and serotonin. They are known as the feel-good chemicals, the ones that drive us to want to return to that feeling. Because of our brain's response, romance can become an addiction. Feasting on "emotional porn" such as romance novels, chick flicks, and sexually themed TV shows sets us up for unrealistic expectations in our real-life relationships.

Researchers estimate that the human brain can only sustain that intense "in love" feeling for a maximum of two years. Ideally, a couple should have worked on deepening their love and commitment during that time so that when the intense feelings of being "in love" taper off, a deeper love takes its place. For those "addicted" to romance, this tapering-off sends signals that it is time to find another person who will induce the same euphoria. Some people diagnosed with "relationship addiction" may, in fact, be addicted to the feelings produced by "falling in love." Thus, they attempt to recreate that feeling over and over again.

With that description in mind, it is easy to see why love and romance are not necessarily the same. The Bible gives several examples of couples who experienced romantic love and the results of those romances. **Genesis 29** tells the story of Jacob falling in love with Rachel. He was willing to work for her father for seven years in order to marry her.

Verse 20 says that those seven years were *"like a few days to him because of his great love for her."* Although Jacob's story continued with deception, heartache, and frustration for everyone, his romance with Rachel is not condemned in Scripture. The story is not the same with Samson. He got into trouble when he let his emotions rule him. **Judges 14** details the beginning of Samson's downfall when he let romance dictate his decisions rather than follow the Lord's direction.

Romance can be either negative or positive depending upon whether we let those emotions rule our lives. When we are pursuing our feelings, we can get into moral and marital trouble. **Jeremiah 17:9** says, *"The heart is deceitful above all things, and desperately wicked: who can know it?"* The popular saying, "follow your heart", is terrible advice. When we follow the passions of our hearts, we are easily led into deception, sin, and regret. Instead of pursuing romance, we should pursue the Holy Spirit's leading in our relationships. It is always wise to pursue love (**1 Corinthians 14:1**). Then, when in the pursuit of showing love someone special rises to our attention, godly romance can be a gift from our heavenly Father (**James 1:17**).

SEX

Sex, the word which has a million synonyms. Unlike our Western counterparts, we do everything to shy away from this topic. It is considered controversial and vulgar. Most Christian youth, aside from teachings on not engaging in any pre-marital sexual act, know next to nothing about it. It is a blessing to keep oneself till marriage. That is what the Lord requires of us all; however, a complete blackout on the subject is not acceptable. It is necessary for would-be couples to read good, godly material addressing sex as God designed it.

When it comes to sex, this is what the Lord expects of us:

"7 Now concerning the things about which you wrote, it is good for a man [a] not to touch a woman. 2 But because of sexual immoralities, each man is to have his own wife, and each woman is to have her own husband. 3 The husband must fulfill his duty to his wife,

and likewise the wife also to her husband. [4] The wife does not have authority over her own body, but the husband does; and likewise the husband also does not have authority over his own body, but the wife does. [5] [b]Stop depriving one another, except by agreement for a time so that you may devote yourselves to prayer, and [c]come together again so that Satan will not tempt you because of your lack of self-control. "

1 Corinthians 7:1-5 (NASB)

Sex was designed by God to be enjoyed only in the confines of marriage, not between two people intending to be married or people who find each other irresistibly drawn to each other. Sex goes deeper than a man and woman involved in a physical act. It bonds two people on a spiritual level. That's why the scriptures say,

"Or do you not know that the one who joins himself to a prostitute is one body with her? For, He says, "THE TWO SHALL BECOME ONE FLESH."

1 Corinthians 6:16 (NASB)

Whoever we have physical knowledge of, we are automatically joined to that person. We open upselves up for a lot of unnecessary spiritual attacks when we have sex indiscriminately with anyone in trousers or skirts. In our time where sex is available with a click of a button, it is extremely important we seek the grace of God to overcome.

For married couples, our bodies are not our own. Our partners own our bodies and we should delightfully seek to pleasure them with it. Mostly, we are eager to explore and pleasure each other in the honeymoon stage of the marriage till the words we never thought we would ever utter sets in. We yield to "I am tired" and I'm not in the mood". Scriptures admonish us not to deprive each other except we both agree to it for a period of time. Immediately after, we are to get together so we do not yield to temptations.

As two individuals with different tastes and preferences, we must understand that our desire for sex will be different. A husband may be more demanding than his wife, or vice versa. It is necessary we find middle ground so that we are not selfish and sex will be something we look forward to. Explore each other's bodies and indulge in conversations aimed at knowing your partner's preferences. Try to be spontaneous and enjoy each other. Some sexual acts are condemnable, though, and we do not encourage them.

Fantasies such as bondage (BDSM), anal sex, orgies etc. are desires which rise against God's design for sex and are harmful to any marriage.

Try to learn new things to spice up your sex life. Do not restrict your sex life to a timetable. This sucks out the joy and pleasure sex is supposed to give. To the Christian wife, do not always wait for your husband to initiate sex. Men love it when their wives yearn for them and make the first move. So please do it more often. It is no sin. Also, dress erotically for your husband. Men are very visual and are turned on by what they behold. If strange women dress to entice men and are successful, what stops you from doing so for your husband? Go all out. Give him something to come home to.

Now to the men, sex is not the same for a woman. Women are likened to a heater whiles men are compared to a stove burner when it comes to sex. This means they have to be conditioned for sex. So take it slowly. Set the mood right. Let her anticipate it and both of you are guaranteed of a wonderful experience.

To sum it up, sex is best enjoyed when we put the needs and satisfaction of our partner above ours.

CHILDBEARING AND CHILDLESSNESS

"Like arrows in the hand of a warrior, so are the children of one's youth. Blessed is the man whose quiver is full of them; they will not be ashamed when they speak with their enemies in the gate." **-Proverbs 127:4-5 (NASB)**

In our part of the world, after the customary marriage and wedding, the next milestone society sets for a newly married couple is childbirth. There are people who keep count of the number of months, days and seconds a couple have been married and are constantly on the lookout for the protruding belly of the wife.

If you think that action is too overbearing, you should watch more Ghanaian and Nigerian movies, especially those with the plot of a mother-in-law who cannot comprehend why her daughter-in-law cannot conceive.

One will cringe at the sheer enormity of verbal, physical and other inhumane attacks such wives are subjected to. To be sincere, It's hard to believe what we witness in such movies. Yet turning a blind eye to the fact that the media mirrors the happenings in society would be a missed opportunity to help resolve societal issues.

Children are precious gifts of God and expressions of our love. They enrich our lives and provide a line of lineage to sustain humanity. Our society places a high premium on child bearing. Most prayers and blessings we hear at marriage ceremonies (both customary and Christian) are "may God grant you many children", "may we meet again at the naming ceremony of your children".

Family, friends and well-wishers will not hesitate to ask why a couple are not conceiving. Some will go the whole length to proffer solutions for a plight which, in most instances, have proved non-existent. Women are those that suffer most from these unsolicited medical consultations. They have to be answering questions from in-laws, friends and sympathizers, drinking concoctions of all sorts and are expected to be open to be present at every spiritual gathering that promises a child.

Men are barely accused of being barren, even in cases when both partners know the problem is from the man. It is always the wife who is labelled barren and subjected to ridicule by any and every one.

Childlessness comes as a huge blow to a couple who have planned their lives and painted a picture of a home where they grow old lovingly caring for their grandchildren. As our elders say, however, in marriage you prepare for the best and expect the worst.

Children are also a status symbol in Ghana and all married adults are expected to have children. In the past, the greater the number of children you had, the higher the respect you earned in the society.

The Frafra people in the Upper East region of Ghana say, "The wealth of a man is not determined by the size of his barn but the number of mouths he feeds." This gives you a rough idea on how important children are in a marriage. We deem it far better to be poor and needy with many children than wealthy without a child.

Marriages without children are, therefore, seen as a bad omen and prone to failure; indeed, in the past, adults who did not have children were deemed to have blocked the line of lineage. They were, therefore, not given a good burial in the hope that their souls would not return to the earth. All couples, therefore, love to have children. However, approximately 70-80 million couples worldwide are currently infertile (Bos et al., 1995; Boivin et al., 2007). They may never experience pregnancy and childbirth.

It should be noted that what we sometimes label childlessness may not necessarily be so. Sometimes a delay in childbirth is hurriedly labelled barrenness. The Bible has many examples of couples who were childless but for the intervention of God. Father Abraham and Mother Sarah were married for many years without a child. We all know how the story went. Sarah, under pressure, gave Hagar, her maid, to Abraham. There is the story of Manoah and his wife (parents of Samson), Elizabeth and Zechariah and many others. Eventually, God showed up in the lives of these couples and He can do same with us in our days too.

Causes of childlessness

Studies show men account for forty per cent of the problems with infertility (University of Utah, Health Sciences Centre). Oh yes! Do you want to go over that line? Please do. This is a sharp contrast to the picture society has painted for us over time. The major problems which besiege men in the area of fertility include impotence, ejaculatory disorders, inability to produce sperms, low sperm count and defective sperms.

Interestingly, women also account for forty per cent of the problem. Their major problems include inability to produce ova, blockage of fallopian tubes, unsafe abortion and fibroid. Aside these health issues which account for couples' inability to conceive, stress and anxiety also play a major role. As the pressure mounts from all sides, many couple gets anxious and restless, which causes more harm than good.

The rest are unexplained or unexpected. There are some cases in which partners are unable to have children but when they separate each is able to have children. Some call it sexual incompatibility.

Effect of childlessness

Unfortunately in our part of the world, Ghana to be precise, it is the woman who suffers most even when she is not the problem. Frustrated and disappointed, she is constantly under stress. She loses respect and may be ridiculed. She is always tense and sorrowful. The risk of being barren can be a heavy burden. The woman risks getting a divorce and in some cases gets rivals.

In extreme cases, women who have been labelled barren are given an ultimatum to give birth or risk being sent out of their matrimonial homes. Women from the extended families, who are supposed to feel for wives in such situations, do the exact opposite and are the crusaders when it comes to tormenting such wives. More of a shocker is when such women are Christians.

The story is told of the leader of the Womens' Fellowship of a Church who beat and dragged her daughter-in law out of her son's house because they could not conceive. Unbelievable!

Some Ghanaian men simply refuse to accept that they could be the problem and the women, in their desperation from social pressures, have been forced to help their men bring in children from outside. This action is an outright insult to the institution of marriage and the vows both parties exchanged.

Childlessness causes constant fights, misunderstanding and suspicion in the marriage.

An otherwise peaceful, loving home becomes a war zone when partners try to outdo each other with hurtful words and actions.

Each partner feels the other is responsible for their childless predicament. Some partners try digging into each other's past and link past events to their recent issues.

Childlessness can potentially take away the joy of lovemaking in marriage. Sex becomes mechanical and unfulfilling: as it is now only an avenue to try for a child. Sex is done strictly in accordance with the wife's fertility window and no consideration is given to the wife and her feeling in the moments of intimacy and lovemaking.

How to deal with childlessness

Childlessness is hard to accept. The first step is to build a positive image of your marriage. Anxiety and pity party will worsen your problem. Do not blame each other or assume a suspicious attitude. Both must cooperate fully. Remember that in this journey, the two of you are a team taking on the world.

It is also important you avoid fake pastors or juju men who will try to convince you that your problem is caused by witches or evil forces. This is very rife in Ghana. Bizarre stories are constantly spewed about married women caught in very uncompromising situations with pastors who claim to be giving them the fruit of the womb. Some go as far as selling off their valuables and cutting off family members they are made to believe are responsible for their childlessness. It is necessary you stay off these so called prophets and pastors.

A couple is assumed to have problems if after two years of regular and active sexual life, there is no pregnancy. It is, therefore, advisable that you have regular sex. Also, appreciate the fact that some women with short or irregular menstrual periods may ovulate during menses. It may, therefore, be advisable to have sex even during their period. There is nothing wrong with it. You wouldn't have broken any taboos. You have the power to part the 'red sea'.

- Every woman is unique. Seek advice and know your body well. Apart from the four common theories on Fertility Awareness Methods, that is made up of standard days method, cervical mucous mothod, basal body temperature and symptothermal method. Recent studies appear to suggest that there are specific days in the year in which a woman in her fertility period can be pregnant. Know your days and act accordingly.

• Avoid herbal concoctions that are not certified by specialists. Most will worsen your condition. Many have been victims of unauthorized concoctions sold on the markets, the recommendations of friends, well-wishers and family. Do well not to take them. Gently turn down these "kind" gestures. Instead, seek medical attention.

Today surgery, hormone treatment and Assisted Reproductive Technology have reduced childlessness but their success depends on factors such as age, health status of couples and even luck. If both partners are up for it, you can opt for in-vitro fertilization and other tech aided means of conceiving.

ADOPTION AND SURROGACY

• If all attempts fail, couples should accept their condition and stay strong. Knowing that you can never have children is not easy but denying it actually hurts more.

• Take interest in other people's children in the neighborhood, social organisation and church. They will benefit from your time and your interest.

• Parenthood is not about biology but about love and care. As you show care and love you become a true model of parenthood.

• You may also develop new interest and get involved in activities like sports club, music and travel to meet people with kids. It helps you to blend in instead of alienating yourself from the rest of society.

• Never think that God does not love you. He has given you what in His perfect plan, is the best for you.

Today we hear of children butchering their parents. God knows your end from the beginning and may be saving you from tragic things you may not know of. If you learn to accept your situation, others will accept you. You don't have kids but you have each other. Cherish and deepen the love you share.

Children are visitors who will come and go. No wonder, studies show that childless couples in later life have higher levels of social participation than older couples who are parents. The love you share with or without children is the only key to a happy marriage.

CHAPTER 8

The Threefold Bond

The Little Foxes That Ruin The Vineyard

"Catch the foxes for us, the little foxes that are ruining the vineyards, while our vineyards are in blossom." -**Songs of Solomon 2:15**

As any married person will tell you, marriage in real life is anything but easy; in fact, for many couples, it can be downright miserable if they don't know how to work through their problems. Think about it, no one teaches us how to have a happy, healthy marriage. If our parents didn't model it for us, then we have no idea how to do it ourselves.

Because of this, almost all marriages have problems. Some couples are better at working through the ups and downs through the years than others, but they all have them. Regardless of whether your problems lead to divorce or you work through them effectively, most married couples have similar issues.

Let's take a look at 15 of the most common problems most marriages face.

1. Division of Labour

Research shows that even when both spouses work outside the home, the woman is usually the one who does more of the housework and chores. Obviously, this creates stress for her, what's even more stressful, beyond these daily chores, is "psychological responsibility." In other words, women are expected to remember things like "Kwame has a doctor's appointment on Tuesday," or "We have to go to Akua's cultural dance performance on Saturday at 2:00."

While it is not always the woman who does more of the work, a lack of balance with labour can cause a lot of issues. When one partner becomes overwhelmed with chores, it gradually leads to resentment.

Partners help each other in every way. There is no chore assigned to one partner. I have seen men who love cooking suddenly stop because they are married.

This should not be the case. If you love cooking as a man, by all means do not stop. Make it a point to help out at home. As a husband, do not sit and cross your legs waiting for your wife to wash, cook and clean. It is hard when you detest doing chores but remember, this is necessary to make your wife happy and keep the home. Start with the little things like taking out the trash, doing the dishes etc. It makes a huge difference.

2. Finances

Some people are spenders. Others are savers. So, if you get a spender and a saver together in a marriage, you can see how that would become a problem.

Maybe growing and investing money is important to one person, but the other couldn't care less about it. Fighting over money and how it is spent is one of the most common problems in marriages. It is of utmost importance to have what is termed the money talk before saying I do. This dispels any assumptions and expectations we have with regards to money. Also in the course of the marriage, the saver should find innovative and Godly ways to encourage the other partner to save.

3. Children and Parenting Differences

Let's face it, raising children can be stressful! The crying/sleepless baby, temper tantrums, and rebellious teenagers are not a lot of fun sometimes, regardless of how much you love your kids. And that can cause a lot of stress to a couple! Even differing parenting styles, like how to punish a child, can cause a rift in marriage. Take turns in nursing the children. It strengthens your bond. Discuss parenting during courtship. Remember to always present a united front to your children. Children are smart and can use a divided front to their advantage.

4. Personality Differences

If one person is an introvert and the other is an extrovert, then there may be constant tension regarding how often to socialize.

The extrovert might feel unloved that the introvert never wants to go to a party with them and the introvert might feel rejected because the extrovert always wants to socialize with people other than their spouse.

This is only one aspect of personality differences that can cause problems in marriages. Knowledge is a treasure here. Study your spouse and relate with them according to their personality and temperament.

5. Fighting and Communication Style Differences

Maybe one spouse grew up in a family where they yelled and screamed at each other when they were angry, while the other spouse grew up in a family that turned their anger inward and would give people the silent treatment. Having different fighting or communication styles when it comes to conflict can be a huge obstacle to having a happy and healthy marriage. The key here is to compromise and figure out which style works for you both.

6. Different Love Languages

Dr. Gary Chapman wrote a book; *The Five Love Languages.* In it, he defines five different ways people give and receive love (acts of service, touch, time, giving of gifts, words of affirmation). If you both speak very different love languages, you might not feel loved by your partner, which may lead to marriage problems. For example, if you want to be given gifts to feel loved but instead your partner would rather do acts of service for you—like fixing your car or rubbing your feet—then you might not understand that they really do love you. Let us strive to identify, understand and speak our partner's love language. We should also be considerate when they do not get it right. It is the thought that counts.

7. Sex

Everyone has different sexual needs—both in frequency and type. Some people love having sex as often as they can, while others could live the rest of their lives without it. Still others need a lot of kinky stuff to be satisfied. Regardless of what you want, most couples have a problem with their sexual compatibility. You are not the first, nor are you the last. Sex is a gift that must be enjoyed. Put each other first and enjoy this beautiful treasure.

8. Jealousy and Infidelity

Many people are naturally insecure and unfortunately, many people are also tempted to cheat on their spouse. So, whether or not someone actually cheats, there can be jealousy that exists within the relationship.

Infidelity isn't limited to physical cheating. Emotional infidelity is running rampant these days because of technology, such as phones and dating apps. They make it so easy to hide what someone is doing and whom they are talking to. Continuous adherence to the Word of God and watchfulness are our only way out of this.

9. Boredom

Relationships are always exciting when they are new. Everyone feels like they are walking on cloud 9 because they are so in love. As time goes on, however, the newness and infatuation wear off. As that happens, many couples fall into a slump. Their relationship stagnates and seems to get boring. It takes effort to try to keep the love alive and to keep doing exciting things together. Revisit the things you loved doing when you were courting - going on trips, cooking together, going on dates. The main reason why marriages get boring is that we stop dating. We like to attribute dating to single people, which is wrong. We should never stop dating our partners.

10. Power Inequity

Power can come in many forms—from financial power to parenting power. If one spouse makes more money than the other (or perhaps one is a stay-at-home parent), that creates an imbalance when it comes to who brings in the money. This imbalance is a common marriage problem. Who has more decision-making power? Many times, it's not equal. That definitely causes problems because one of the spouses could start to feel powerless over time. Empower your partner. Remember that we are life partners supposed to help each other fulfill our God-given purpose. Give your partner some autonomy.

11. Abuse

Abuse comes in several forms. Physical abuse is what most people think of when they hear the word abuse, but mental and emotional abuse is as detrimental. When one or both persons do not respect the other but resorts to laying hands on the offending party or using horrible language when they speak, that can tear apart a marriage in no time. We are of the view that abuse, once meted out, has the tendency to become a habit. We advise to steer clear of abuse in any form. It is simply unhealthy.

12. Values and Beliefs

As the saying goes, "a bird and a fish may love each other, but where will they live?" In other words, when two people have very different world views, it makes it difficult to understand each other, and this may lead to problems in marriage.

For example, if a Catholic is married to a Muslim, they probably don't share a lot of beliefs and worldviews. Similarly, when one is a Republican (or NPP) and the other a Democrat (NDC), that can cause major tensions in marriage as well.

13. Trying to Change Each Other

No one is perfect. There will always be something about everyone in the world that will annoy you. When people don't understand this they try to change each other. They think, "I can't stand that Bob doesn't want to go to the gym and work out with me, but when we get married, I'll change his mind." No. That NEVER works! You cannot change people. We cannot change people but we may change for people. Changing here means acceptance. You should just learn to accept each other the way they are; otherwise, you will be making each other miserable with all of the naggings that go into trying to change a person.

14. Keeping Score

When someone feels like they are doing way more for the other person than they are for them, it's natural that they will keep score. The wife may think, "I work, and then I come home and cook and clean and take care of the kids. But all the while, Ben is just sitting on the couch, drinking his beetroot juice, and not even noticing how stressed out I am!".

In her mind, she has racked up a lot more on the scoreboard than he has. As a result, resentment builds up over time and can ruin a marriage. In this situation, communication is key. This helps because your partner may not necessarily know you are keeping score.

15. Unrealistic Expectations

We all have an idea how we want other people to act, especially our spouses.

For example, you may assume that when someone is married, they should have sex every day. They overlook the reality that most couples are tired from work, taking care of the children, chores, etc. That is an unrealistic expectation: in real life, it doesn't happen.

Maybe you think your wife should cook gourmet meals all the time just like your mom did. Well, maybe she hates to cook! Putting unrealistic expectations on your spouse will only get you both frustrated and angry. Just as you cannot fulfill all the expectations of your spouse, do not expect the same. Cut your spouse some slack.

THE THREEFOLD BOND

HUSBAND+WIFE+HOLY SPIRIT

"And though a man might prevail against one who is alone, two will withstand him—a threefold cord is not quickly broken." – **Ecclesiastes 4:12 (ESV)**

From the very beginning of our conversation, we have repeatedly talked about our union being different from others. The basis of Christian marriage is and will always be the Word of God. The perfect model for us is Christ and his marriage to the Church.

In the preceding chapter, we spoke of the many issues that may arise or attack the sanctity of marriage. To overcome these and enjoy our marriage as God designed it, we need the extra cord. The personality of the Holy Spirit is a great ally for married couples. He is the third person who can help us work out our differences and live in harmony.

Simply put, the equation for the threefold bond is Husband+Wife+Holy Spirit. Without the Holy Spirit, it is not possible. It is in our human nature to keep score. It is natural to seek our pleasure above others. It is normal for us to compete with each other. This is where the Holy Spirit comes in so that we can love as Christ loved us.

No couple sets out to get married to get divorced later on. No one wants to waste their emotions, time, money and resources and separate a few months later.

It is alarming the rate of divorce in our generation now. Let us face it, being a nice person doesn't guarantee a beautiful marriage. We have the nicest man or woman becoming the worst husband or wife to their partner. There are some things that we have no control over. We will have to submit it to the Lord trusting he will work in us to be Godly spouses. For our threefold bond to stand, our twofold strand must be closely knitted in the salvation and knowledge of our Lord Jesus Christ.

For Christ to be at the centre of our marriage, He must first be at the centre of our individual lives. For most of us, we assume having a wedding automatically means we have a threefold bond. How far that is from the truth! We should have our personal relationship with Christ first. Then we can hinge our relationship on our mutual knowledge of Christ. This makes it possible for us to have a strong threefold bond

KILL 'SELF'

To have a strong threefold bond, it is imperative that we kill self. Self here refers to our desires, our pleasures. The most common word in marriages that breeds trouble is the word 'I'. A root analysis of issues begins from what we want for ourselves with little or no regard for what our partners want. Mostly when we start speaking from a place of me, we put on a stance of attack. It blinds us from satisfying our partner's needs and wants. We are only concerned with what we want and nothing else. We fail to see reason with our partner.

Isn't it interesting the many times we compromise at our various places of work but refuse to go out of our way to do the same for our partners? The same person we vowed to spend the rest of our lives with? The same person we exchanged vows with in the presence of man and God!

The model on which our marriage is hinged is a grand display of sacrifice. Jesus left his throne, majesty, grandeur and splendour to die for his bride, the Church. Now look at the scenario: the Church is not even pure but Christ is ready to sacrifice all and goes on to make the Church clean and presentable unto Himself. To succeed in this this institution called marriage, we need to continually be in tune with the Holy Spirit and please the Holy spirit. This is what makes it easy to sacrifice and put the joy of your spouse first because the Holy Spirit enables you to do so.

GET KNOWLEDGE

"The beginning of wisdom is: Acquire wisdom; and with all your possessions, acquire understanding." – **Proverbs 4:7 (NASB)**

There is a profound statement by renowned author, Dr. Myles Munroe. It says, ***"Love is not the foundation for a marriage"***.

This singular statement sparked a string of conversations, with many agreeing and disagreeing with him. We were not so sure where we belonged, but upon reading more, we realized what he said was the truth.

Every divorced couple were once in love. Every couple have been in love. Even in relationships that didn't work out, love was involved; therefore, to build your marriage only on love is not very wise. What makes it more alarming is what we classify or define as love. For many couples, the beginning stages of marriage, characterized by euphoria, tingling and lightheaded feeling are guarantee that we are in for the long haul. Unfortunately when this feeling leaves us, we begin to second guess our choices. That is when our inadequacies and lack of preparation start showing.

As we grow, it is expedient we arm ourselves with knowledge. Some go to great lengths to get the perfect wedding dress, dresses that no eyes or mind can fathom, because they must be the first to wear them. We have seen young men toppling over each other to get married to the prettiest girl alive. Sad to observe, these same people are in no hurry to acquire knowledge about the life journey they are about to embark on.

There is an African proverb that says, "Not to know is bad; not to wish to know is worse." We cannot afford not to know. It is only but a matter of time before our lack of knowledge in this area glares us in the face. For an institution that gives out certificates before you enroll in the course, we need all the knowledge we can gather.

Having said all of the above, invest in books and other literature which will enrich your knowledge. Thanks to the internet, we have access to a lot of information.

Let's download sermons, buy books on marriage which will build us up for the journey of marriage. To most of us the only marriage we have seen is that of our parents. Depending on how it was, we would have varying perspectives on what our marriage should be. It is necessary we learn from other scenarios and experiences aside what we are used to.

There are people who are of the opinion that books are only theory and cannot prepare you well enough. This is not fact. We are better equipped to handle situations we have read about than those we have no idea of. We will urge us to continue reading, keep watching those helpful videos. Go for programmes that will enhance your knowledge. You will be better off.

References

1. U.S. Census Bureau, Children's Living Arrangements and Characteristics: March 2011, Table C8. Washington D.C.:2011.

2. Elizabeth Tandoh, Contemplating Getting Married? 2017.

3. Bishop Dag Heward Mills, Model Marriage: A Marriage Counselling Handbook: 2015.

4. https://www.childtrends.org